CHEMISTRY

FLAMES
Are Stored
SUNLIGHT

Dr. Bryson Gore

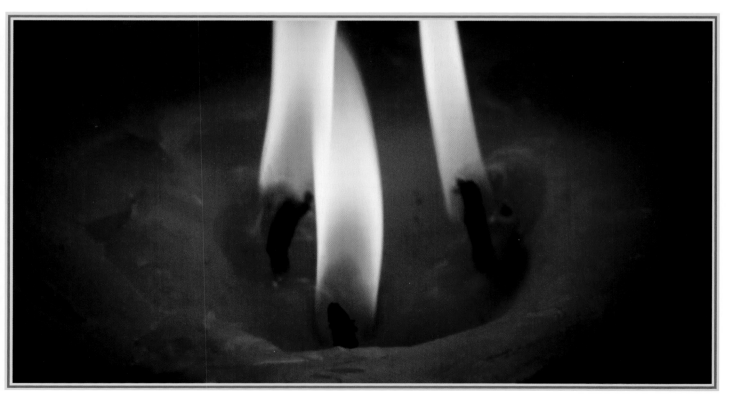

Stargazer Books

CONTENTS

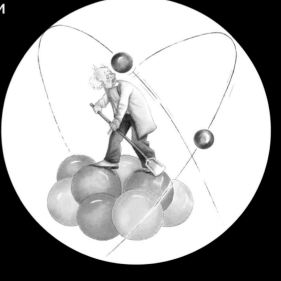

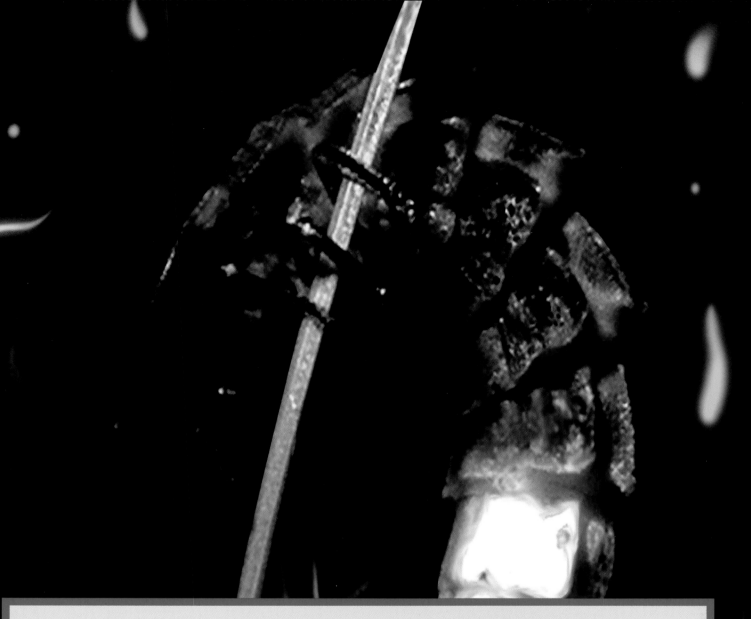

© Aladdin Books Ltd 2006

Designed and produced by
Aladdin Books Ltd

First published in the
United States in 2006 by
Stargazer Books
c/o The Creative Company
123 South Broad Street
P.O. Box 227
Mankato, Minnesota 56002

Printed in Malaysia

Editor: Katie Harker
Design: Flick, Book Design
and Graphics
Illustrators: Q2A Creative
Picture research: Alexa Brown,
Katie Harker, Flick Smith

The author, Dr. Bryson Gore, is
a freelance lecturer and science
demonstrator, working with the
Royal Institution and other
science centers in the UK.

Library of Congress Cataloging-in-
Publication Data

Gore, Bryson.
   Chemistry / by Bryson Gore.
    p. cm. -- (Wow science)
   Includes index.
   ISBN 1-59604-066-1
   1. Chemistry--Juvenile
   literature. I. Title.

QD35.G685 2005
540--dc22
                    2005041808

Introduction

Humans have puzzled over CHEMISTRY—the study of substances —for hundreds of thousands of years. What am I made from? Why does cooked food taste nice? What happens when a metal gets rusty? In the last 300 years, we have answered these and many other questions by studying the material world and how it changes.

In ancient times, people believed that the world was made from mixtures of the "four elements"—Earth, Air, Fire, and Water. Then, around 1000 A.D., alchemists began to experiment with substances by heating and mixing them together in search of the "philosopher's stone"—an unknown substance thought to have the power to turn cheap metals, like lead, into expensive ones, like gold! Although the alchemists failed, their experiments laid the foundation for modern chemistry.

About three hundred years ago, the era of the alchemist drew to a close and modern chemistry began. Alessandro Volta and Luigi Galvani uncovered the link between chemistry and electricity by inventing and developing the battery. Other chemists studied the composition of rocks and minerals and chemists slowly realized that there were not just four elements but dozens! In the 19th century, Dimitri Mendeleev worked out how to catalog these elements and to predict the existence of additional elements.

In the 20th century, biologists needed the skills of chemists to help them to understand "proteins"— giant molecules that form the building blocks of living materials. Today, chemists also use the "ingredients" from Mendeleev's Periodic Table to build molecules that have never existed on Earth before.

This book takes a look at twelve of the most amazing chemical discoveries that have taken place through history. Find out more about famous chemists like Mendeleev, Maillard, and Avogadro, and learn how they used their skills to make sense of the chemical world. By consulting fact boxes such as "The science of..." and "How do we know?" you will begin to understand more about the ways in which we have pieced together the story of elements, atoms, and molecules. Learn about the power of energy, the composition of materials, and the way in which different substances react—that together explain the changes that we see in the world around us.

MERCURY IS THE ONLY LIQUID METAL

Everything in the world around us is made from elements: substances composed of minute particles called "atoms." One group of elements —called "metals"—are usually thought of as strong, hard materials used to make great buildings. But some metals possess quite different properties. Iron will melt if we make it hot enough, sodium is soft enough to scratch with your fingernail, and gallium will melt in your hand. Mercury is an unusual metal because it is liquid at room temperature.

THE SCIENCE OF...

Thousands of years ago, people recognized that there were millions of different types of material in the world. They guessed that there were a smaller number of basic materials—elements—that couldn't be broken down into simpler substances, but could combine to make the materials that we see around us.

Scientists now know that there are about 110 different elements in the universe—and that everything on Earth is built from around 80 of them. One of the most important tools in chemistry is the "Periodic Table" (see p.30) —a list of elements that has been arranged to group similar types together.

Roughly two-thirds of elements are metallic—shiny, silvery, and good conductors of heat and electricity. Metals on the left of the table, like sodium (Na) and potassium (K), are very reactive and can explode on contact with water. Less reactive metals, like iron (Fe) and gold (Au) (right), are in the center while non-metallic elements, like carbon (C) and oxygen (O), are on the right-hand side of the table.

HOW DO WE KNOW?

In 1869, a Russian chemist named Dimitri Mendeleev proposed what we now call the "Periodic Table." Mendeleev didn't know why elements differed (see p.9), but he knew about properties—like the weight—of different elements. Although scientists couldn't weigh individual atoms, they could measure the atomic mass relative to hydrogen (which was assigned a value of "one"). Experiments using batteries split molecules into individual atoms so that they could be compared.

Mendeleev set about drawing a table that had the lightest element, hydrogen (H), in the top left corner and the heaviest element in the bottom right. He started a new line every time he came to an element similar to hydrogen and found that this pattern meant that other elements with similar properties appeared on top of each other. It's the fact that these properties repeated themselves periodically as the weight increased that gives the table its name.

Dimitri Mendeleev was not the first chemist to see that there were patterns in the properties of the elements, but he was the first to believe that these patterns were important.

SCIENTISTS CAN TURN LEAD INTO GOLD

For hundreds of years, alchemists, the forerunners of modern chemists, tried to turn lead into gold, but they never succeeded. Today, we understand that chemistry cannot turn one element into another. However, in the 1980s physicists managed to change a few thousand atoms of lead into gold for the first time in history. Their secret was the use of a nuclear reactor.

THE SCIENCE OF...

Chemists now recognize that everyday substances are formed when elements combine to form molecules and compounds. The atoms in compounds and molecules are held together by chemical bonds, and chemists have discovered that it is the movement of electrons within and between atoms and molecules that creates these chemical bonds. Although chemistry can change which atoms are bonded together, it cannot change the identity of an atom.

For many years, alchemists tried to change cheap elements like lead into expensive ones like gold—but they never succeeded! Chemical reactions couldn't do that but in 1980, a particle physicist called Glenn Seaborg used high-energy particles from a nuclear reactor to split the nuclei of lead atoms. The nucleus of a lead atom has 82 protons while the nucleus of a gold atom has 79 protons. By forcing each lead atom to release three protons, they turned into gold. This process needed an enormous amount of energy so Seaborg's gold was far too expensive to produce commercially, but he showed that scientists, at last, could achieve what alchemists had failed to do.

HOW DO WE KNOW?

Around 100 years ago, scientists began to look inside atoms in an attempt to discover what makes one element different to another. Using beams of radioactive particles (called "Alpha" particles), they found that almost all of the mass of an atom was concentrated at its center, called the "nucleus." The nucleus was compiled of protons and neutrons, surrounded by a cloud of electrons giving the atom its size and shape.

Neutrons have no charge and electrons are negatively charged. Since atoms are neutral we can therefore deduce that the protons in the nucleus have a positive charge that counteracts the charge of surrounding electrons.

Physicists have now shown that the nucleus CAN be changed using radioactivity. Radioactive substances have a nucleus that spontaneously disintegrates or decays, emitting high-energy particles. When an atom is radioactive or when it is bombarded by particles from a nuclear reaction, some of the protons can be removed from the nucleus, altering the composition of the atom in the process.

SIX ELEMENTS MAKE UP 99% OF YOUR BODY

Everything in the world around us is made from elements—and so are we! Chemists can detect microscopic amounts of almost every known element in the human body but we now know that just six types of elements make up around 99 percent of your mass and the atoms in your body.

Elements in the human body
Six elements are responsible for the majority of your mass and atomic structure.

◁ **Calcium** 1.5% mass
0.25% atoms

Hydrogen ▷
10% mass
63% atoms

◁ **Carbon**
18% mass
9.5% atoms

Phosphorous ▷
1.0% mass
0.20% atoms

◁ **Oxygen**
65% mass
25.6% atoms

Nitrogen ▷
3% mass
1.35% atoms

Calcium is essential for the development of strong teeth (above) and bones.

HOW DO WE KNOW?

The work of doctors, scientists, and nutritionists has helped to uncover the composition of the human body. We now know that more than half of our body is composed of water (H_2O)—with hydrogen and oxygen being the most common atoms in our body.

Your body also contains about 20 percent fat, which mainly consists of hydrogen and carbon atoms. Although eating too much fat can be bad for you, some types of fat are necessary to build your cell walls and to protect your brain cells (which are mostly made from fat). Your muscles are made from protein fiber containing hydrogen, carbon, oxygen, and nitrogen and your bones and teeth are made from calcium phosphate.

Eating a balanced diet helps maintain the composition of your body. You can help to redress the balance if you are deficient in a particular element by eating certain foods or by taking vitamin or mineral supplements.

THE SCIENCE OF...

To keep our body in good working order we need to provide it with a continuous supply of the "top six" elements. **Hydrogen** and **oxygen** are components of water and most other compounds. Oxygen gas is also essential for respiration. **Carbon** is one of the main "building blocks" of living organisms. **Nitrogen** is found in proteins, nucleic acids, and other compounds. **Calcium** is important for membrane function, nerve impulses, muscle contractions, and blood clotting, as well as being the main component of bones and teeth. **Phosphorous** is found in the structure of bones and teeth, nucleic acids, and other compounds.

Your body has a selection of many other elements in small amounts—such as potassium, sulfur, sodium, and magnesium. These elements are also vital if the body is to function properly. We help to replenish our body with these important substances by eating a balanced diet. Protein, fat, sugar, and carbohydrates contain the elements carbon, hydrogen, nitrogen, and oxygen. Dissolved salts contain calcium, carbon, oxygen, and phosphorus. Potassium and sodium are also found in table salt.

THE SCIENCE OF...

Two of the most important groups of chemicals in science are the "acids" and "alkalis." Strong acids and alkalis will react with a wide range of natural materials, dissolving rocks and even turning fat into soap! Acids and alkalis are also now used to make candles (right) because they help to create a long-lasting wax.

Acid is the name we give to chemicals that release electrically-charged hydrogen atoms, called "ions," when they dissolve in water. Alkalis are the chemical opposites of acids and react strongly with acids to produce water and different compounds, depending on the acids and alkalis used. For example, hydrochloric acid and sodium hydroxide (an alkali) react to produce water and salt—sodium chloride.

The strength of acids and alkalis is measured using a scale called pH—positive hydrogen ion concentration—an indication of how many hydrogen ions are dissolved in the water solution. The strongest acids have a pH of around zero, pure water has a pH of 7, and the strongest alkalis have a pH of around 14. The acid in your stomach has a pH of about 2, which means that it's a pretty strong acid!

How do we know?

Acids have been known about by chemists for hundreds of years and prized because of their ability to react with many types of rocks and ores. The most important acids that are used in industry are hydrochloric acid (HCl), sulfuric acid (H_2SO_4), and nitric acid (HNO_3). These are known as inorganic acids because they are produced from rocks and ores that we find around us.

Animals and plants make inorganic acids like HCl, but they also make "organic" acids. Vinegar (ethanoic acid) is produced when wine is allowed to "go bad" as bacteria feed on the alcohol (ethanol), turning it into an acid. Formic acid (methanoic acid) is the irritant in ant bites and bee stings.

Many years ago, cooks discovered that some natural dyes change color in acid and alkaline solution. The red colors of beetroot or blackberries are natural indicators of pH. In acid solutions the dyes are red, and in alkali they turn blue. Later, chemists used "Universal Indicator"—a mixture of natural indicators that gradually change color from strong acid (red) through neutral (green) to strong alkali (purple)—or "litmus paper" (a similar indicator obtained from a type of fungus known as lichen). Today, chemists are more likely to use electronic pH meters to measure the strength of acids and alkalis directly.

ACID IN YOUR STOMACH CAN "BURN" ROCKS

Chemical reactions are needed to break down the food we eat so that it can be used by our bodies. Our stomachs contain one of the most powerful acids known to start this process. Stomach acid is so strong that it is able to "burn away" rocks like chalk and limestone.

FLAMES ARE STORED SUNLIGHT

When a flame burns, it releases the chemical energy that is stored in the fuel that is burning. But where does that energy come from? All chemical fuels on Earth originate from plants, and because plants convert light energy into chemical energy, the energy of a flame originally came from the light of our sun.

HOW DO WE KNOW?

All of the chemical fuels that we have on Earth are derived from plant materials. These fuels contain energy that has been stored through the process of photosynthesis.

Plants have to convert light energy into chemical energy in order to survive. Photosynthesis facilitates this by combining carbon dioxide and water to form carbohydrates (which the plants need to grow) and oxygen (which the plants release into the atmosphere).

The energy that we get from the sun is astounding—every hour more energy falls on the earth as sunlight than mankind uses in a year! Plants store that energy in the form of carbohydrates, and over millions of years the energy is also converted into different "fossil fuels."

Fuels like coal, oil, and gas were formed millions of years ago when large areas of forest grew and were later buried under shallow seas. The layer of seawater prevented oxygen from the atmosphere reaching the forest material so the plants did not decompose. Instead, they became trapped beneath newly-formed sediment on the seabed. Today, we have to drill through the earth's surface to recover these fossil fuels.

THE SCIENCE OF...

All chemical reactions either absorb or release energy. A flame is a sign that a chemical reaction is giving out a lot of energy because we can see and feel the very hot gases produced as the chemical reaction occurs.

When a plant is growing, energy from the sun's light is used to drive the process of photosynthesis (see p.14). When a plant sheds its leaves (or dies), it decomposes by combining with the oxygen once more. As photosynthesis occurs it releases exactly the right amount of oxygen into the atmosphere to burn all of the plant material produced. Photosynthesis also removes the same amount of carbon dioxide from the atmosphere that will be released when a plant is burned. The burning of fossil fuels, however, removes oxygen from the atmosphere and releases carbon dioxide—but no oxygen is replaced.

The color of a flame gives a good indication of the type of fuel that is burning. The blue flame from gas comes from the burning of hydrogen atoms. The orange-yellow flame of a candle (right) comes from the burning of carbon. Carbon-based fuels also release tiny particles of carbon, called "soot."

THE SCIENCE OF...

Satellites and space stations
get their power from three main sources.
Large, flat solar cells, or "photovoltaic" cells,
generate electricity directly when sunlight falls on them.
Sometimes, however, the earth will be positioned between
the space station and the sun, and so energy needs to be stored.

In space stations, raw materials are often used to make fuel cells—
water is split to make hydrogen and oxygen gases that are stored and
later combined in a fuel cell to generate electricity. The water produced
as a byproduct of these fuel cells can also be used as fresh drinking
water for the crew! Satellites do not have room to store gases so,
instead, rechargeable batteries are used—similar to the battery used
in a cell phone (right). Electricity is forced through the battery to
reform the fuel (metal) that stores the electrical energy.

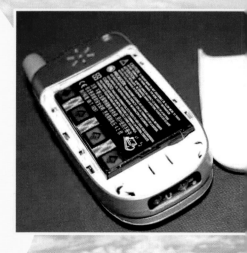

SPACE STATIONS ARE POWERED BY BATTERIES

You probably know that spacecraft are launched into space using thousands of tons of fuel, but once they are there, where do they get their power from? Today, satellites and spacecraft—like shuttles and the new international space station—use solar cells to generate electricity. However, they also use batteries and fuel cells to store and supply energy when it's needed.

HOW DO WE KNOW?

The chemical battery was discovered over 200 years ago by two Italian scientists called Alessandro Volta and Luigi Galvani. Galvani noticed that dissected frogs' legs would jump if they were hung from a copper wire. At first, Galvani believed that the "life force" of the frog must be causing the movement. However, Volta then discovered that if you hung the copper wire from an iron bar, electricity was produced. Galvani and Volta had made a simple electrical (or "voltaic") cell—it was actually electricity that had made the frogs' legs twitch!

This discovery showed that if two metal wires touch in water, one metal dissolves in a chemical reaction that drives electricity around the wire circuit. Galvani and Volta's finding also helped to show that all chemical reactions involve the movement of electricity within and between reacting molecules. Modern batteries are a type of voltaic cell—the fuel (metal) is stored in the battery until it is needed. Fuel cells differ from voltaic cells because the "fuel" is supplied from the outside, usually in the form of a gas.

A chemical reaction happens when bonds between atoms and molecules are made or broken. Chemical reactions use energy to carry out these processes, which are often irreversible. The energy used in cooking reactions is usually heat, but when chemists work they also use electricity, light, or even the energy stored in other chemicals.

We often melt and freeze food in cooking, but this is a reversible (rather than a chemical) reaction. It would be difficult to unmix dough, but no chemical change takes place until the heat from an oven causes chemical reactions to occur (below). The chemical reactions that make bread, cake, meat, or vegetables brown are called "Maillard Reactions" after Louis-Camille Maillard, a French chemist who discovered in 1912 that sugars and proteins reacted together when heated to produce brown products. Decades later, food scientists discovered that these brown molecules had strong, and often pleasant, flavors.

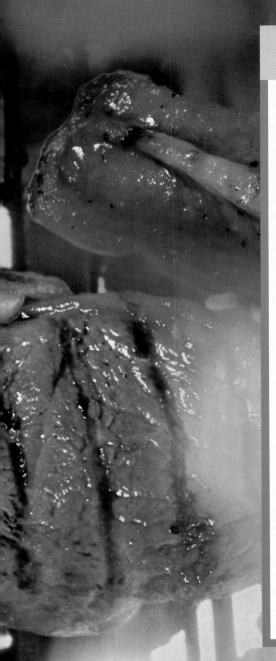

For thousands of years, great cooks produced delicious food without understanding the chemistry involved. Today, we realize that a good cook has to understand as much about how molecules combine and change with heat as a chemist working in a laboratory!

We know that many cooking techniques involve chemical reactions because they make permanent changes to the ingredients that we use. Many different chemical reactions can take place in the kitchen. Here are just a few examples:

• Toffee is made by gently heating sugar in a pan. As the sugar combines with oxygen from the air, the sugar molecules join together and become brown. This is a gentle form of burning, and we often say that toffee tastes of burnt sugar.

• Sponge (or "honeycomb") toffee is made by adding vinegar (an acid) and baking soda (a mild alkali) to hot toffee. The acid and the baking soda chemically react to release carbon dioxide (see p.12), and the bubbles of gas are trapped in the sticky toffee as it cools.

COOKING IS A CHEMICAL REACTION

Many cooking techniques involve mixing ingredients together to enhance flavor, but mixing isn't itself a chemical reaction. When we heat food to cook it, real chemical reactions cause changes that cannot be undone. Next time you take a mouthful, think about the chemical reactions that have caused your bread to turn brown or your toffee to taste different to sugar.

HOW DO WE KNOW?

Although air may look like empty space, it actually contains an incredible number of molecules! Air is made up of about 80 percent nitrogen and 20 percent oxygen. Using Avogadro's Number (see p.21), we know that one Mole of air (or any gas) contains about 6.02×10^{23} particles. That's 602,000 million, million, million molecules! One Mole of nitrogen (N_2) weighs about 28 g and one Mole of oxygen (O_2) weighs about 32 g. Taking an approximate average of these weights shows that one Mole of air weighs about 30 g.

Avogadro discovered that one Mole of gas occupies about 25 liters at room temperature and pressure. With this knowledge we can deduce that one cubic meter of air (1,000 liters) contains about 40 Moles of molecules. If one Mole of air weighs about 30 g, then 40 Moles of air weighs about about 1.2 kg, or 2.6 lbs! As you walk around each day, there is a huge weight above your head! We call this "atmospheric pressure." Luckily, the pressure of our bodies counteracts this weight, so we don't feel it.

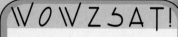

WOWZSAT!

CHEMISTS CELEBRATE "MOLE DAY" ON OCTOBER 23RD, FROM 6:02 A.M OR 6:02 10/23. THE TIME AND DATE ARE DERIVED FROM AVOGADRO'S NUMBER (6.02×10^{23})— THE NUMBER OF MOLECULES IN A MOLE.

HERE IS A HUGE WEIGHT ABOVE YOUR HEAD

You may be surprised to discover that the air weighs anything at all! But did you know that every cubic yard or meter of air contains about 27 million, million, million, million molecules? In order to talk about large numbers like this chemists have invented the "Mole"—a word that stands for an enormous number! One cubic yard or meter of air is said to contain about "40 Moles" of molecules.

THE SCIENCE OF...

In the 19th century, Amedeo Avogadro was a chemist who studied how many atoms were in a liter of gas. By looking at the way in which different gases combined chemically, Avogadro discovered that one liter of any gas, at the same temperature and pressure, contains the same number of particles—this is known as "Avogadro's Law." For most gases, like nitrogen and oxygen, those particles are molecules made up of two or more atoms bonded together.

Avogadro found that 1 g of hydrogen had the same number of atoms as 12 g of carbon. This was determined to be roughly equal to 6.02×10^{23} and is known as "Avogadro's number." Today, scientists usually refer to this as one "Mole" of atoms. A Mole of different substances weigh different amounts. For example, one Mole of aluminum weighs 26 g of aluminum. So, an aluminum drinks can (below) weighing about 15 g contains about half a Mole of aluminum atoms.

HOW DO WE KNOW?

When a metal rusts, although the surface of the metal looks like it is being worn away, the metal atoms are actually combining with oxygen from the air. Iron oxide is the chemical name for the brown "rust" that forms on old iron structures.

Antoine Lavoisier was the scientist who first realized that when chemicals react together their total mass always remains the same. Lavoisier showed that although atoms in molecules are rearranged when they change states from a gas to a liquid, or a liquid to a solid, they are never destroyed.

There are, however, some substances that lose mass when they combine with oxygen. When coal oxidizes (burns) it loses atoms to the air (as carbon dioxide gas) and becomes lighter. Although chemical reactions rearrange atoms they never make or destroy them.

WHEN OBJECTS RUST THEY GET HEAVIER

When metals rust they appear to lose their shiny surface and slowly disintegrate. Atoms on the surface of an old iron car or boat combine with oxygen atoms from the air to produce a surface coat of iron oxide—or "rust"! This chemical reaction means that, rather than losing atoms, metals actually gain atoms when they rust and decay.

WOWZAT!

GOLD IS AN UNUSUAL METAL BECAUSE IT DOES NOT FORM AN OXIDE IN AIR. THIS IS ONE REASON THAT GOLD IS SO VALUABLE. GILDED OBJECTS WILL REMAIN THEIR NATURAL GOLD COLOR FOR MANY YEARS WITHOUT TARNISHING.

THE SCIENCE OF...

Most metals tarnish if they are exposed to the air for a long time. One of the most common examples is iron which tarnishes, or rusts, if left exposed to air. Water also encourages this reaction by dissolving oxygen and iron so that they react together.

Sodium and potassium are shiny bright metals, but they rust so quickly that if you leave them in the air overnight they will have rusted away by the morning! In fact, these metals combine with oxygen so powerfully that they even react with the oxygen atoms in water. To keep sodium and potassium shiny, they have to be covered in oil and stored in airtight jars.

Oxygen is not the only atom that metals can combine with. Over time, copper reacts with sulfur in the air to form a green substance called copper sulfide. Buildings and statues are often covered with copper so that they eventually tarnish to this attractive green color (left). However, rust isn't always colored. Aluminum oxide is a white molecule—when it forms on the surface of aluminum it isn't easily visible at first.

A LOT OF METAL IS FOUND IN OCEAN WATER

Take a sip from a glass of water. Is it pure? It might taste like there's nothing but water in the glass, but you may be surprised to know that there's probably over a tenth of a gram of solid dissolved in every liter! This is what gives water its taste.

THE SCIENCE OF...

Anyone who has swum in the ocean knows that water is salty. "Salt" is the common term for any compound of a metal with a nonmetal. Seawater has about 80 lb (36 kg) of different types of salt dissolved in every cubic yard or meter of water. Most of that is sodium chloride (table salt) but about 3 lb (1.5 kg) is made up of magnesium atoms, with another 1 lb (0.5 kg) of both calcium and potassium.

If we evaporate seawater we are left with a white solid that is a mixture of the different salts. Chemicals that react with metals are often used to isolate a single salt, but simply passing electricity through the salts can also isolate the pure metals that are present. For example, when sodium chloride is electrolyzed it produces sodium metal and chlorine gas. Today, sodium chloride (table salt) is obtained by mining underground layers of salt and by drying out seawater.

Water from a faucet or bottle also contains salts—from rocks that the water has dissolved from the ground. You can find a list of the salts dissolved in a bottle of mineral water by reading the label (right). Mineral water contains relatively low levels of sodium chloride but often has higher levels of calcium and carbonate —the chemical name for chalk!

How do we know?

You will notice that the taste of water changes in different locations. When rainwater first falls to the ground, it doesn't contain any salts. However, as this water seeps through the ground, it dissolves rocks like limestone and chalk. As a result, rainwater will contain dissolved mineral salts when it flows into the ocean, or when it eventually reaches our homes through a faucet. Metals also find their way into the oceans and into our water supply. When discarded metal objects rust they dissolve in the water around them, to eventually be carried into the oceans, or our homes.

Why doesn't the ocean just get saltier and saltier? Geologists believe that this is because water in the sea is slowly filtered through very hot rocks deep under the floor of the oceans. Here, the dissolved salts form solid rocks that, one day, may return to the earth's surface to be washed away by the rain.

However, some seas contain different amounts of material. Although the average ocean contains about 3.5 percent solid, the Dead Sea in Israel contains salt concentrations as high as 27 percent! The Dead Sea is land-locked and because it has no connection to other oceans of the world, the water and mineral salts that flow into the Dead Sea just stay there. In the heat, the water evaporates leaving mineral salts that slowly crystalize and fall to the bottom of the sea. The high concentration of salts also means that the Dead Sea is very dense—this makes it easy for people to float in the water!

WOWZSAT!

SEAWATER CONTAINS MINUTE AMOUNTS OF MOST METALS. THE OCEANS CONTAIN ABOUT 0.000,004 G OF GOLD PER CUBIC METER. THIS MAY NOT SOUND VERY MUCH, BUT IT MEANS THAT THERE IS ABOUT 5.5 MILLION TONS OF GOLD IN THE OCEANS!

HOW DO WE KNOW?

Most of the atoms in the world around us, and in our own bodies, are in the form of molecules—atoms stuck together with chemical bonds. Many molecules only contain a few atoms but polymers are unusual because they contain thousands, or even millions, of atoms bonded together. Long-chain molecules are formed by stringing together hundreds or thousands of simpler molecules—a bit like the beads of a necklace.

Over the past 50 years, polymers made from the molecules in crude oil have been the basis of the manmade plastics industry. A number of simple molecules—like ethylene—are used as the starting point for most modern plastics. If chemists string hundreds of ethylene molecules together they make polyethylene (polythene). If each ethylene molecule has a chlorine atom attached to it, they produce Polyvinyl Chloride (PVC) and if each ethylene molecule has a benzene molecule attached, it's called polystyrene.

A RUBBER MOLECULE CAN STRETCH TO OVER FOUR TIMES ITS NORMAL LENGTH

Have you ever wondered why a rubber band is "stretchy," and other things like the rubber of a car tire are not? Many "natural" materials like wood or oil are made from long molecules that contain thousands of atoms stuck together. Manmade plastics are often similarly enormous. But it's how a material is stuck together that determines whether it is stiff or stretchy.

THE SCIENCE OF...

Rubber is a biological molecule made naturally by rubber trees. Carbohydrates, proteins, and fats are examples of other molecules found in animals and plants. Biological molecules tend to be in the form of long-chain molecules (right).

A single rubber molecule is a long, thin chain composed of hundreds of thousands of atoms. The molecules in a rubber band (or the bands of a bungy rope) are loosely tangled around each other in loops and coils. When you pull on the rubber band, the molecules straighten out so that the band becomes longer. Once the molecules are straight the rubber becomes very stiff. Car tires are made from rubber that has been chemically treated with sulfur. The sulfur links different rubber molecules together so that they can't move past each other. They will stretch, but to a lesser extent.

Different trees produce different biological molecules. Pine trees produce sap, or resin, that contains short-chain molecules that make it very sticky. Over time, the chains become linked by the oxygen from the air to make a hard clear

A fire gives out light because it is hot. As the carbon and hydrogen of the fuel combine with oxygen, the flames and embers are heated by the energy released. The embers are red hot, about 1,800°F (1,000 °C), and the flames can be even hotter. Although a firefly can create a flash of light from within its body, no animal could survive having that sort of temperature inside it. Instead, these animals use chemistry at "room temperature" to give out light.

Fireflies (lightning bugs) and glowworms are probably the most famous examples of animals that produce light. However, as scientists have descended into the depth of the oceans they have also found many different fish that illuminate their surroundings and communicate using a process called "chemiluminescence." A number of species of jellyfish do this—and angler fish use their ability to make light to attract other fish so that they can eat them! Chemists have learned how to replicate the chemiluminescent tricks of nature—have you seen light sticks and necklaces (right) used at celebrations and festivals?

HOW DO WE KNOW?

All chemical reactions absorb and release energy. In the laboratory this energy is usually in the form of heat. Living creatures are not able to survive at very high temperatures, but scientists have discovered that if molecules are held in fixed positions as they react, it can dramatically reduce the temperatures needed for a chemical reaction.

Different enzymes are used to control almost every chemical reaction that takes place inside animals and plants. Enzymes are a group of molecules that act like scaffolding—they support

other molecules as they react, and can control the speed at which those reactions happen. Scientists have discovered that fireflies use an enzyme called "luciferase" that links to another molecule called "luciferin." When luciferin burns in oxygen it doesn't lose its energy to its surroundings as heat, but instead emits energy as a single flash of light.

As chemists come to understand how effective enzymes are at facilitating reactions at low temperatures, they are starting to use them themselves in the laboratory and in industry.

ANIMALS CAN MAKE COLD LIGHT FROM CHEMICALS

We're used to seeing hot objects like a fire or lightbulb give out light, but did you know that some plants and animals can glow in the dark without burning themselves? Their secret is to use enzymes—special molecules used by all living creatures to make reactions work at body temperature.

WOWZSAT!

During the Second World War, Japanese pilots used to carry packets of dried fireflies. By adding water to a little of the powder in the palm of their hand, they could produce enough light to read a map at night.

Glossary

Acid—A liquid with a high concentration of hydrogen ions.

Alchemy—The ancient practice of trying to turn cheap materials into expensive materials.

Alkali—A liquid with a low concentration of hydrogen ions.

Atom—The smallest piece of an element.

Battery—A device that turns chemical energy into electrical energy.

Bond—A link between two atoms.

Chemiluminescence—A chemical reaction that gives out light at low temperatures.

Compound—A chemical made up of two or more atoms.

Dissolve—When a solid mixes completely with a liquid.

Electron—A negatively-charged particle that surrounds the nucleus of an atom.

Element—A substance that contains only one type of atom.

Enzyme—A protein that controls the speed of a reaction.

Inorganic—Materials produced from rocks.

Ion—An electrically-charged atom or molecule.

Mole—A unit used to describe very large numbers of atoms and molecules.

Molecule—Two or more connected atoms.

Nucleus—The center of an atom.

Organic—Materials produced by plants and animals.

Oxide—The compound formed when an element reacts with oxygen.

Periodic Table—*see below.*

Photosynthesis—A process that plants use to convert sunlight into chemicals.

Polymer—A long chain molecule that is made by combining smaller molecules.

Radioactive—Radioactive substances have a nucleus that spontaneously disintegrates or decays, emitting high-energy particles.

Periodic Table—A diagram (below) that lists all the elements based upon their chemical properties.

1▷	H	3▽												1▽			6▽	He	◁ 7
	Li	Be											B	C	N	O	F	Ne	
2▷	Na	Mg	4▽										Al	Si	P	S	Cl	Ar	
	K	Ca	Sc	Ti	V	Cr	Mn	Fe	Co	Ni	Cu	Zn	Ga	Ge	As	Se	Br	Kr	
	Rb	Sr	Y	Zr	Nb	Mo	Tc	Ru	Rh	Pd	Ag	Cd	In	Sn	Sb	Te	I	Xe	
	Cs	Ba	La	Hf	Ta	W	Re	Os	Ir	Pt	Au	Hg	Tl	Pb	Bi	Po	At	Rn	
	Fr	Ra	Ac	Rf	Db	Sg	Bh	Hs	Mt	Ds	5△								

1. Non-metals 2. Alkali metals 3. Alkaline earth metals 4. Transition metals
5. Metals 6. Halogens 7. Noble gases 8. Rare earth elements

8▽

Ce	Pr	Nd	Pm	Sm	Eu	Gd	Tb	Dy	Ho	Er	Tm	Yb	Lu
Th	Pa	U	Np	Pu	Am	Cm	Bk	Cf	Es	Fm	Md	No	Lr

Biography

Amedeo Avogadro (1776-1856) An Italian chemist whose study of gases revealed important findings about atoms and molecules.

Luigi Galvani (1737-1798) An Italian anatomist whose early experiments contributed toward the discovery of electricity.

Antoine Lavoisier (1743-1794) A French scientist who is often regarded as the "father of chemistry." Lavoisier discovered that when chemicals react, their total mass remains the same.

Louis-Camille Maillard (1878-1936) A French scientist who discovered a reaction between sugar and protein that changes the color and flavor of food.

Dimitri Mendeleev (1834-1907) A Russian chemist who devised the Periodic Table.

Glenn Seaborg (b.1912) An American scientist who changed lead into gold, by means of a nuclear reaction.

Alessandro Volta (1745-1827) An Italian scientist who invented the Voltaic cell—the first electric battery.

KEY DATES

1780—Luigi Galvani carries out experiments using electrical charges.

1800—Alessandro Volta designs the first electric battery.

1811—Amedeo Avogadro studies the amount of atoms in a particular volume of gas and determines a constant, now known as "Avogadro's Number."

1869—Dimitri Mendeleev proposes the "Periodic Table"—a list of elements with similar types grouped together.

1912—Louis-Camille Maillard discovers that sugars and proteins react together when heated to produce brown products.

1980—Glenn Seaborg successfully turns atoms of lead into atoms of gold, using a nuclear reactor.

Index

Photocredits: l-left, r-right, b-bottom, t-top, c-center, m-middle.
Front cover c, 14-15—Digital Vision. Front cover bl—Corbis. 1m, 15r, 16b, 18ml, 24br—Flick Smith. 2-3, 28-29—David Godwin/Q2A Creative. 4bl, 24-25—Stockbyte/Q2A Creative. 4br, 22-23—Corel. 5t, 8-9—Flat Earth/Q2A Creative. 5tm, 26-27—African Extreme. 5m, 18-19 Corbis/ Flick Smith. 5bm, 20-21—Darren Holloway/Q2A Creative. 6br—World Gold Council www.gold.org. 11tl—Image Library. 12m—Select Pictures. 16-17—NASA/Flick Smith. 21br, 23bl—www.freeimages.co.uk. 27br—Q2A Creative. 28tr—www.glowcolours.com.